LONDON'S BLACK CABS

a Pocket History

Bill Munro

First published 2024 by
Earlswood Press
10 Chaldon Close
Redhill
Surrey RH1 6SX
www.earlswoodpress.co.uk

Copyright © Bill Munro 2024

The right of Bill Munro to be identified as the author of this work has been asserted in accordance with the Copyrights, Designs & Patents Act 1988
All rights reserved. No part of this book may be reprinted or reproduced or utilised in any form or by any electronic, mechanical or other means, now known or hereinafter invented, including photocopying and recording, or in any information storage or retrieval system, without permission in writing from the publisher.

ISBN 978-0-9957308-8-5

Typeset in Minion Pro 10pt by Earlswood Press
Printed and bound in the UK by TJ Books Limited, Padstow, Cornwall

LONDON'S BLACK CABS

a Pocket History

Contents

Acknowledgments — 6

Why the Name "Black Cabs"? — 7

Introduction — 9

1 Before there were "Black Cabs" — 13

2 The First "Black Cabs" — 23

3 The Rise of the Austin FX4 — 35

4 The Dominance of the Austin FX4 — 47

5 The Creation of LTI and the Arrival of MCW's Metrocab — 53

6 The Fairway, more Metrocabs and the Asquith — 63

7 The LTI TX-Series and the LEVC TX — 73

The Public Carriage Office — 87

Further Reading — 92

Acknowledgments

This book is largely based on my previous works, *A Century of London Taxis* (Crowood, 2005), *London Taxis: a Full History* (Earlswood Press, 2011 & 2014) and *The London Taxi* (with Nick Georgano, Shire, 2011), suitably updated to take in the new generation of electric cabs that have appeared since 2018 and abridged to fit a far smaller format than either *Century* or *Full History*. I have taken the liberty of re-using many of the photographs in my collection. This is out of necessity, as the number of photographs of London cabs on the streets is low. I have, hower managed to locate a number of previously unused images, which hopeflyy bring fresh look.

Nick Georgano's *A History of the London Taxicab* (David & Charles, 1972) was the first book on the subject to be written after the Second World War. This was followed in 1976 by Philip Warren & Malcom Linskey's *Taxicabs: a Photographic History* (Almark, 1976). These two books provided a foundation for my own research and I will always be indebted to the authors for their research.

I derived a great deal of the information I have used from interviews with many people in both the cab trade and in taxi manufacture, including Bill Lucas, Peter James, Grant Lockhart, Barry Widdowson, Jevon Thorpe, Peter Wildgoose and Andrew Overton from Carbodies and Mann & Overton; Geoff Chater and Bob Parsons from MCW; Roy Ellis, Ray Biggs and Jack Everitt from the Public Carriage Office and Geoff Trotter and Roger Ward from the London General. There are many more whose names I have left out for lack of space and I apologise for doing so, for I owe you all so much. "Thank you" seems hardly adequate.

Bill Munro, Surrey, 2024

Why the Name "Black Cabs"?

The answer might seem obvious. They are cabs, and they are black. And you might think they had been called that since cabs first appeared, but as the third generation of my family to be involved in the London cab trade, I can tell you they haven't. I first came across the expression in the early 1980s, when I heard it used by a minicab driver. Like many of his contemporaries, he had ambitions to do The Knowledge of London, the tough test that all London cab drivers must take if they are going to drive a taxi for a living. He referred to it as "doing his black cab".

The minicab business hijacked the term "cab" from the licensed cab trade when they began operations in the early 1960s and in the minds of the public the word became generic for both taxis and minicabs, despite it being illegal for minicab companies anywhere in the UK to use the word "cab" in descriptions of their business. And indeed the Public Carriage Office, the body that was then responsible for licensing London's taxis and taxi drivers until they were taken over in 2000 by Transport for London, never used the word "taxi". They always used the word "cab". When London's private hire trade (a minicab is, in law a private hire vehicle) was licensed in 2000, the licensing authority became Transport for London, Taxis & Private Hire and the word "taxi" became official parlance for the first time. And though "black cab", started as a slang, almost derogatory term, it has entered general use and has even been adopted by the longest-serving manufacturer of London taxis, LEVC Ltd in Coventry.

There has never been a contract given to a single company to make London taxis. Any motor manufacturer can do so, but it is such a small market that only two companies, or groups of companies have dedicated themselves to it. One, which began with Napier cabs in the 1900s and was taken on by Beardmore, Metro-Cammell-Weymann and finally, KamKorp, is no longer in the business. The most successful is that which began with Mann & Overton's Garage in Edwardian times, commissioning cabs from Unic and then Austin, until becoming absorbed by London Taxis International, before that organisation in turn became LEVC Ltd.

And do they have to be black? The answer is, quite categorically, "no". London's cabs can be any colour – there has never been a regulation dmanding that they be painted black – and black is by no means a universal colour for London's taxis. The first London cabs to be painted black appeared in the 1940s, as this book will reveal.

We must go back four centuries to understand the full story of the vehicles and how they came about, but before we move on, let's get rid of one old chestnut. There has never been a law or rule that requires a London taxi driver to carry a bale of hay in his cab. A horse cabman had to carry sufficient hard feed to keep his horse fed during a shift, but that law was never applied to motor cabs!

Introduction

London's taxis, the famous "Black Cabs" are unique, but why? Quite simply, it's because of the rules that govern the trade and how the cabs are constructed. But what are those rules, and how did they come about? To find the answers to these questions, we must start our story in London at the beginning of the sixteenth century. Then, London was a small, walled city. Its streets were narrow and filthy and the most convenient way to travel within the city was on foot, or to move from one end to the other by hiring a boat along the River Thames.

During the sixteenth century, London's population began to grow and the people that could, moved outside the old Roman walls into the surrounding villages and parishes, including Westminster and parts of Middlesex. Wealthier people moved westward and to the northwest, away from the filth of the city and the smoke and stench that was blown eastwards by the prevailing winds. Now they were living further away from their friends and often some distance from the river. They needed wheeled transport to travel any distance and that came in the form of the hackney coach.

The coach originated in Europe in the sixteenth century and made its appearance in London in the latter part of that century. Coaches were very expensive and thus were bought by the wealthy, but they were costly to keep, requiring a coachman, a groom and horses to pull them. To help pay for it all, the owners began to hire the coaches out to those with aspirations of, or perhaps pretentions of grandeur. When the older vehicles began to wear out, owners bought new ones and sold the old ones, often to innkeepers, who had stables and yards in which to keep them. The innkeepers hired them out on short term hire, for either a single journey or perhaps for a day or a half day and from this the coaches acquired the name hackney coaches, after the old Norman French word, "haquenée", meaning a horse for hire. By the beginning of the seventeenth century, the streets of London and Westminster were clogged with these cumbersome two-horse vehicles. The people of London, especially other road users began objecting to them, calling them "hackney hell-carts". Some individuals petitioned the king, unsuccessfully, to rid London of them.

The first semblance of order for the hackney coach trade came in 1634,

A hackney coach, by London's Temple Bar. The illustration gives little idea of the bulk and the weight of these early coaches. (Author's Collection)

from a retired sea captain, Captain Baily, who placed four coaches at the Maypole in The Strand, just outside the boundaries of the City of London. He dressed his coachmen in a smart livery and instructed them to charge set fares to various destinations. At a stroke, Baily set up a business model that exists in the cab trade world-wide to this day. Baily's practices were soon copied but did not provide a solution to the congestion.

The people who kept these coaches, the hackney coachmen, petitioned King Charles I for some sort of licensing to try to restrict the numbers and thus protect their income. The king, however had more pressing matters to deal with and it was his nemesis, Oliver Cromwell who first brought in the Ordinance for the Regulation of Hackney Coachmen in 1654. It was the first act of parliament under Cromwell's Commonwealth, but it soon lapsed and it was not until 1694, in the reign of William III and Mary II that hackney coaches were first properly licensed. This was brought about under the "Act for the lycenseing and regulateing Hackney-Coaches and Stage-Coaches". It was supervised and enforced by the newly formed Office of the Hackney Coach Commissioners, who licensed the coaches and the owners, though not the drivers. This regime lasted until 1843, when the Metropolitan Police was given control of the trade. By this time, the hackney coach was rapidly being replaced by the cheaper, single horse cabriolet, the name of which was quickly shortened to "cab".

Hackney coaches and their drivers were, quite rightly, criticised, because the coaches were often in deplorable condition and the drivers were ill-mannered, dishonest and frequently intoxicated.

Shortly before the Metropolitan Police took over, the Hackney Coach Commissioners licensed the drivers and gave them badges to wear, which the drivers hated. The Metropolitan Police enforced discipline rigorously and ensured that the drivers wore their badges and behaved in a responsible manner. Towards the end of the nineteenth century the police set up driving tests and, in Edwardian times, medical examinations. Most importantly for our story, rules were soon set out governing the way that cabs should be constructed, including the materials used and the dimensions of the seats and the police kept firm control on how the cabs were maintained and on the welfare of cab horses. The framework was thus established for the arrival of motor taxicabs.

An 'outrigger' cabriolet from the 1820s. The advantages of the vehicle are to the benefit of the operator and, to some extent, the passenger, but not in any way for the driver! (Author's Collection)

Chapter 1

Before there were "Black Cabs"

London's first two-wheeled cabs were replaced by improved designs, including the 4-wheeled "growler" and the more famous 2-wheeled Hansom cab, both of which appeared in the early 1840s. They soon became common sights in Victorian London.

The Bersey Electric Cab

In the 1880s in Germany, two men, Karl Benz and Gottlieb Daimler, working independently of each other, produced the world's first practical motor cars. Both men soon put their inventions to work as *automobildroshken*, or motor cabs.

Although in Britain the ownership of motorised road vehicles was legal, using them on public roads was totally impractical, as the Locomotives Act of 1865, the so-called "Red Flag Act" restricted the maximum speed of a mechanically propelled carriage to two miles per hour in towns and demanded that the vehicle be preceded by a man on foot, carrying a red flag to warn of its approach. This of course deterred all but the most dedicated of enthusiasts.

Such a group of men were determined to make owning and running motor cars practical, which meant getting the Red Flag Act repealed. In 1896 they succeeded and set up a factory, the Motor Mills in Coventry to make motor cars. One of the first vehicles was a licence-built Daimler car and the other was an electrically-powered cab, named the Bersey, after

A Hansom cab in London's Bond Street. (Author's Collection)

A Bersey electric cab with, it is believed, Walter C. Bersey himself at the wheel. (Author's Collection)

its designer, Walter C. Bersey. More than thirty Berseys were put to work on London's streets from 1897. Despite the public's initial curiosity, press hostility and the unexpectedly high cost of running the cabs brought the company down. They were withdrawn by the end of 1900 and from then until 1903, horse-drawn cabs continued to serve the capital.

The First Motor Cabs

In 1903, the London Express Motor Service Ltd obtained consent from the PCO to put three French-built Prunel motor hansoms on test. After a satisfactory trial, they were withdrawn, the company was reformed as The Metropolitan Cab & Carriage Company and capital was sought, unsuccessfully to finance a much bigger cab fleet. Another pioneer, the London Motor Cab Company was set up before Metropolitan, with less than a dozen Rational motor hansoms. A few others, such as The Motor

A Prunel motor hansom of the Express Motor Service Ltd. ranks up at Hyde Park Corner in 1903, behind Hansom two cabs. (Stanley Roth Collection)

15

Hansom Company followed, but likewise on a small scale, for there was no appetite amongst investors for the motor cab business. By 1905, fewer than 19 motor cabs were running on London's streets.

The General Cab Company

Then a sea change occurred, through the formation of the French-backed General Cab Company of Brixton, South London in 1905. They introduced 500 Renault landaulet cabs, similar to those operated by their Parisian counterpart. The size of the operation gave investors confidence in the future of the motor cab business and between 1905 and 1914 the number of motor cabs rose to over 7,000 as new enterprises, some of them quite substantial companies, started by motor manufacturers like Rover and FIAT or those with dealerships, like W&G du Cros sprang up. Over forty different makes of motor cab were seen at one time during this period, whilst the number of horse cabs fell from 11,000 to just 1,300.

Mann & Overton's Garage

But despite the number of makes around, it was not a car maker or proprietor that came to dominate the trade, but a car dealership, Mann & Overton's Garage. Based in Pimlico, it was formed in 1898 when John J. Mann and Tom Overton began importing cars from France and Germany. In 1905 they sold their first cab, a French Unic 10/12hp. Like the Renault it had a 2-seater landaulet body, which by this time had ousted the hansom type for motor cabs.

The Conditions of Fitness

The role of the Public Carriage Office, a part of the Metropolitan Police, was as guardian of public safety. Its head, Supt Arthur Bassom commissioned the Metropolitan Police Regulations for the Construction and Licensing of Hackney (Motor) Carriages (1906), otherwise known as The

Conditions of Fitness, to ensure that all motor cabs were properly constructed and kept in a safe operating state. Introduced in the spring of 1906, the rules, updated over the years, remain in place today and they make the London taxi, the "black cab" what it is. The Conditions of Fitness specified the most notable feature of the London taxi, its 25-feet (7.62-metre) turning circle, which is still in force.

The Unic 10/12hp, however did not meet the turning circle requirement. Though existing cabs were allowed to continue in use, Mann & Overton's had to cease selling new ones and they commissioned a new Unic, the 12/16hp that was designed to meet

A Renault cab of the type imported by the General Cab Company. There is no windscreen fitted and at first, there wasn't even a roof over the driver! (Author's Collection)

the regulations. This more powerful vehicle, which could carry a 4-seater body, became the most numerous make of cab in London prior to the First World War.

Changes in Regulations

The London Cab & Stage Carriage Act of 1907 set the configuration of cabs that exists to this day. Early motor cabs had a seat beside the driver, but this was banned under the Act, for fear of a passenger deliberately interfering with the controls. Another clause in the Act made the fitting of a taximeter compulsory. Until this time, cab fares were printed in a book and cabmen had to memorise them. Disputes between cabmen and passengers over the fares a cabman demanded were the single biggest reason why cabmen were brought before magistrates and the introduction of the taximeter cut those disputes down considerably. The introduction of the taximeter also brought a new term – taxicab. This was first coined by an American, Harry N Allen in 1909 for his New York City fleet of cabs and, abbreviated to "taxi" it quickly became universal.

But then a series of events brought about the collapse of the large, corporate cab fleets that had come to dominate the London trade. Then, and until 2000, London's cab fares were set by the Home Office. When the big companies first set up in business, they based their costs on horse cab fares of one shilling (5p) a mile. When the taximeter was made mandatory, the Home Office decided to set a lower tariff for motor cabs, to encourage people to use them. That tariff had a starting fare ("flagfall") of 8d (4p) plus 8d per mile. At a stroke, this cut the proprietors' revenue by a third, making their businesses, with their substantial overheads, unprofitable. They could hire out their vehicles on a private basis per day and set their own rates, but there was simply not enough work to compensate for the losses. The London Motor Cab Proprietors' Association requested a tariff increase, but the Home Secretary refused. A further blow came when petrol, which the fleets were providing to the drivers, rose to 1/1d (5.25p) per gallon. Most of the big fleets closed and sold off many of their cabs to their drivers, some of whom, not having the huge overheads of the big companies, were able to build up their own small cab fleets. Mann & Overton's Garage, being a dealer rather than a proprietor, was the big beneficiary of this change in circumstances, selling to owner drivers and small fleet owners. By the outbreak of the First World War, Mann & Overton's Unic 12/16 was the only new cab available to the London cab trade.

The First World War took a heavy toll on the London cab trade, as it did on Britain as a whole. With most of the taxis on the road being of French make, spares became unobtainable as the French motor industry turned its attention to munitions production. After the Armistice, cabmen returning home from military service found it hard, if not impossible to find a cab to work as so many vehicles had been lost and not replaced.

A Unic 12/16 cab, taken for a Sunday outing. Before the end of the Second World War, Cabmen were unusual in being working-class men who had motor vehicles at their disposal. (Laurie Chandler)

The 1920s & 1930s

Scotland's largest industrial concern, William Beardmore and Company began work on its own make of cab in 1915. Making its debut in 1920, it was well built and reliable and it gained the nickname, "The Rolls-Royce of cabs". By the end of the 1920s, over half the cabs in London were Beardmores. In 1922, Mann & Overton's reintroduced an updated Unic 12/16hp and there were several other new makes, including the Anglo-Canadian Hayes, the heavy and underpowered Mepward, the American-made Yellow Cab and the cheap and reliable Citroën 11.4hp. None, though were as popular as the Beardmore or the Unic.

But why were there so few makes, compared to over forty that had been seen before the war? Motor vehicle design had vastly improved and the cost of the more popular car makes like Morris and Austin had fallen, but the Conditions of Fitness had remained unchanged since 1906 and no manufacturer made any model that could be modified to comply and be sold at a price acceptable to the trade.

Mann & Overton's publicity image of an Austin 12/4 LL, or "Low Loading" cab, with a Jones body, made from 1934 to 1938. Though car styling changed considerably during the 1930's, London cabs retained the landaulet style body. (Author's Collection)

Above: the Austin FL, nicknamed the "Flash Lot" was the last model of the 12/4 series, made from 1938 until 1940. It shared the LL's chassis, though the body had more modern styling. It was the first pre-war Austin to have a window in the driver's door. (Author's Collection)

Below: the Morris-Commercial G-Type was the first London cab to be made by this company. It was introduced in 1929 and stayed in production until 1932, by which time 1,700 had been made. (Author)

Finally, in 1928 the Conditions of Fitness were relaxed, to try and attract new makers. The biggest and most important change was a reduction of the minimum ground clearance from 10 inches to 7 inches, though the 25ft turning circle remained. Four new models appeared, the Morris-Commercial G-Type, the Beardmore Hyper, the Unic KF1 and the Austin 12/4. The Austin was based on a version of the 12/4 car chassis, modified to meet the Conditions of Fitness and was commissioned by Mann & Overton's as a replacement for the obsolete Unic. Cheap to buy, reliable and backed up by Mann & Overton's service, the Austin 12/4 quickly and comprehensively outsold its competitors. Throughout the 1930s, Britain's largest motor manufacturers, including Austin, moved over to the use of all-steel bodies, but this type of construction requires an investment that can only be economical if cars are built in their tens of thousands a year; the largest number of new London taxis sold in one year during the 1930s was 1,515, in 1934, so the bodies had to be traditional coachbuilt ones. These, for the Austin came from Strachan, Jones Brothers, Goode & Cooper and Vincent's of Reading.

A further reduction in the ground clearance allowed the new "LL" or "Low Loading" Austin to be licensed. This became by far the biggest selling model of the 1930s. The landaulet body common to London taxis had a dated appearance, but it was easily recognisable by the public, whatever the make. That shape, originating in Edwardian times evolved gradually to that of the vehicles we have today.

Chapter 2

The First "Black Cabs"

Motor car design and manufacture changed rapidly during the 1930s, with improved production methods bringing prices within the reach of many more people. The number of cars on Britain's roads doubled from around 1 million in 1930 to 2 million in 1939. Immediately after the Second World War, the motor industry reintroduced a selection of their pre-war models because their new models were not ready for production. The makers of London taxis, however had no old models with which to restart production, because the plant and machinery to make them had been scrapped.

The Nuffield Organisation, owners of the Morris-Commercial brand had built a prototype cab, the Oxford in 1939, which was put on test throughout the war by Beardmore Motors. It was quickly put into production in 1947 and Beardmore's, who had no new model of their own, became the dealers and distributors for it. The body for the Oxford cab was of traditional composite construction, with pressed steel panels over a wood frame and it was built in the Nuffield Organisation's Morris Bodies Branch in Coventry. At the time, steel was severely rationed by the government and the quantities allocated to car makers depended on the export potential of their cars. Nuffield received Beardmore Motors' steel allocation and this enabled them to build the cab without using up their own supplies.

The original Nuffield Oxford cab, photographed near Regent's Park in the winter of late 1947. The pre-war type Sankey steel artillery wheels were chosen because they accommodated the special heavy-duty taxi tyres. (Roy Perkins)

The Oxford's appearance was an evolution of pre-war models, retaining the open luggage platform and separate wings. The PCO, though, had banned the landaulet body, so the Oxford had a fixed roof. The PCO's reason for this change is that they wanted cabs to look more like modern cars, though retaining a "demarcation between car and cab". The open luggage platform was kept, not because the Conditions of Fitness specifically demanded it, but because there were minimum dimensions for it and fitting a fourth door to a vehicle with separate wings and running boards would make the luggage platform too small.

The Oxford had an overhead valve 4-cylinder petrol engine of 1.8 litres, mated to a 4-speed gearbox. The running gear included a beam front axle and despite Nuffield fitting hydraulic brakes to their private cars in the 1930s, the Oxford had mechanical brakes. This was not because the Conditions of Fitness required this older technology. The PCO's vehicle inspectors, known as Carriage Officers, were guardians of public safety and would be held responsible if anything they approved was found to be the cause of serious injury or loss of life in a passenger. Thus they were painstaking to a fault in approving innovations and cab manufacturers chose to remain with specifications they knew were tried and tested and would be approved with little delay, rather than spend time and money trying innovations that might take months to be accepted.

Where pre-war cabs were painted in various colours, commonly maroon or blue or, occasionally, green, with black wings, the Oxford was finished all over in standard black cellulose, to keep production costs down rather than because it was required by law; in fact there has never been a law demanding that London's cabs be black. The Oxford was released at the Commercial Motor Exhibition in October 1947 and went into production in 1948. Though it would not be coined for at least another quarter of a century, this was the origin of the term "Black Cab".

The Austin FX3

The Austin 12/4 taxi ceased production in 1941, so when the war ended, Austin produced a new taxi chassis for Mann & Overton. Numbered the FX, it had a 1.8 litre sidevalve engine but in tests both chassis and engine proved inadequate, so a second chassis, the FX2, with a 1.8 litre overhead valve petrol engine was developed. Austin could make the chassis, but they had not the production capacity to make and fit the bodies, especially as there was a government directive to the motor industry for as many cars as possible to be produced for export. Thus Austin needed all the production capacity and steel at its disposal. Fortunately, Austin's bodywork engineer Joe Edwards knew a company that could help. It was Carbodies Ltd of Coventry, to whom they had subcontracted the manufacture of aircraft fuselage panels during the war. Through the Lend-Lease scheme, Carbodies had acquired Kirksite, a low melt alloy from which cheap press tools could be made, which was used to press the aircraft parts. This would enable Carbodies to make an all-steel body for the FX3 at an economical price. Edwards got together with Carbodies and Mann & Overton and between them they put together a plan, where Mann & Overton would fund half the cost of design and manufacture and Carbodies and Austin split the balance between them. The arrangement was that Austin supplied chassis to Carbodies, who would build the body, fit it to a chassis, paint it and trim it and deliver it to Mann & Overton, who would be the sole London dealer. This was an historic arrangement that secured the future of the London taxi for both the capital and the trade nationally.

Then, in a change of model policy, Austin abandoned the 1.8 litre engine and a 2.2 litre version was installed in the third taxi prototype, the

The Austin FX2 prototype, which carried a coachbuilt body, put together for type approval by the PCO. Austin chose to use disc-type wheels rather than the antiquated Sankey artillery type, but at first, the PCO would not allow the use of hubcaps, fearing that they may conceal loose wheel nuts, or worse, that some may be missing. (WCHCD Archive)

Mann & Overton's brochure picture for the Austin FX3. There was no rule in the Conditions of Fitness that required the luggage platform to be open. The width of the platform, however was set by the rules and that meant that, with bodies with separate wings, it would be impossible to fit a fourth door. (Author's Collection)

FX3. This was introduced at the 1948 Commercial Motor Show and put into production. It was priced at £936/1/8d (£936.09). Like the Oxford, the FX3 was offered in a standard black paint and retained the 3-door configuration of pre-war cabs, although it was fitted with a sliding glass screen on the driver's nearside to give some weather protection. Later models had an optional heater for the driver, which was luxury indeed! A chassis-cab was also offered for special bodies, the most common types seen being London newspaper vans, hearses and couturiers' gown vans. Around a half dozen wood-bodied shooting brakes were also built on the chassis.

Above: an early Austin FX3 outside Buckingham Palace. Later models would feature the familiar roof-mounted "limpet" indicators. (WCHCD Archive)

Below: This preserved FX3 is an early, 1949 petrol model. The maroon overspray was applied originally in 1953 to commemorate the coronation of Her Late Majesty Queen Elizabeth II. (Author)

Above: one of a small number (possibly six) of shooting break bodies mounted on either an Austin FX3 or FL1 chassis. The FL1 chassis differed from that of the FX3 in having a larger, 37ft turning circle. (Author)

Below: this newspaper van, built on an FX3 chassis was operated by United Motor Services on behalf of London Evening Standard newspapers. (Author's Collection)

Double Purchase Tax

The prices of both the FX3 and the Oxford were inflated by the addition of 33.3 per cent purchase tax, which was imposed on luxury goods during the Second World War. Purchase tax, though was doubled to 66.6 per cent in 1950 to help fund Britain's participation in the Korean war and this, coupled with a rise in the base price put the cost of the FX3 to over £1,300. Worse for the FX3 was its fuel consumption of 18mpg. The cab was both too expensive to buy and to run and this was made even more difficult for the trade by the fact that London's cab fares had not been increased since before the war and inflation had sent prices to an unprecedented level. Sales of the FX3 and the Oxford plummeted and it became an economic necessity for cab proprietors to hang on to their pre-war cabs for as long as they could, just to stay in business.

The Diesel Revolution

In 1951, London cab proprietor John Birch discovered the new, 2.1-litre Standard diesel engine that was being fitted in the Ferguson tractor. Though it only produced 21bhp, Birch thought the engine was worth testing in an FX3, to try and improve the fuel consumption. This would at least make the FX3s already on the road economical to run, even though nobody was prepared to pay the price of a new one.

He contacted Arthur Freeman Sanders, the engineer who had developed the engine and had him produce a more powerful road-going version. It was fitted into one of Birch's fleet cabs and although it was noisy and slow, it returned 35mpg. This, plus the fact that diesel fuel was very much cheaper at the time than petrol, the conversion at last made the FX3 economical to run. Birch went on to convert hundreds of FX3s, mostly for fleet proprietors, until Austin produced a diesel engine of their own. This outsold the petrol version by ten to one. The diesel engine, along with the black paint, set a pattern for London taxis that would last until the early 21st century.

The Removal of Purchase Tax on Cabs

In 1953, cab trade representatives got purchase tax removed from London type cabs and from then on, sales of FX3s increased dramatically. At last the old pre-war cabs were retired, with some being exported to the USA and others sold off to students as cheap, spacious transport.

The Beardmore MkVII "Paramount"

Beardmore Motors was doing well out of selling and servicing the Oxford, but the doubling of purchase tax brought sales to a virtual standstill and the British Motor Corporation, a merger of Austin and Nuffield Organisation, scrapped the cab. Beardmore then developed a new model of their own, the MkVII "Paramount". Like the FX3 and the Oxford, it was of a traditional, 3-door design, although with a coachbuilt body with aluminium panels, built by Windover. It was powered by a Ford Consul engine and was the first London cab in production with hydraulic brakes. The PCO insisted that these, for safety reasons were dual-circuit. The MkVII was introduced in 1954 and, like the FX3 and the Oxford was offered in a standard black finish, although an overspray in a choice of red, ivory or blue was available at extra cost.

John Birch (on the right) and his engineer, Sidney Stewart with the first Austin FX3 to be converted to diesel power. (Peter Birch)

A Nuffield Oxford Series III, introduced in 1951. It replaced the Series II of 1950, which featured the 'Easicleen' wheels seen here. The Series III is further distinguished by the extra side windows. (Roy Perkins)

When Windover went out of business in 1958, production of the Beardmore taxi was taken over by Weymann at Addlestone, Surrey. Sales were nowhere near that of the FX3 or even the Oxford, though the marque had its own small, but dedicated following.

The Birch "Essbee"

Following on from his diesel conversions, John Birch produced a revolutionary prototype cab, based on a specially built version of the Standard Vanguard chassis. Its body style was modern, being the first London taxi with four doors, but its seating and door arrangement was unique. Three passengers sat on the back seat and a fourth sat facing rearwards, along-

Above: A 1956 Beardmore MkVII, with the original type Windover body. The front wings are, like the rest of the body made of aluminium. (Author)

Below: What might have been. The Birch "Essbee" cab was built on a special Standard Vanguard chassis. The body was built by Park Royal Vehicles Ltd of West London. (Peter Birch)

The Birch Essbee's luggage compartment was accessed by this full-height door. (Peter Birch)

side the driver but separated from him by a partition. Luggage was carried in a rear compartment, accessed by a full height door in the nearside rear quarter. It went into service in 1955 for a short period, but never went into production.

Chapter 3

The Rise of the Austin FX4

Towards the end of the 1950s, London's taxis, with their separate wings and open luggage platforms were looking very dated alongside some of the sleek modern cars on the road. That was about to change, with the arrival of the FX3's successor, the Austin FX4. To design and build it, Mann & Overton chose to continue their successful partnership with Austin and Carbodies, with Austin beginning work on it in 1956.

The styling of the FX4, with its full width body was conservative rather

This sketch by Austin design draughtsman Eric Bailey was the one best liked by Mann & Overton's board. Though details were changed, the general design was adopted for the production vehicle. (Barney Sharratt/Author's Collection)

Above: One of the first production Austin FX4s. The straight door handles would prove fragile and were soon replaced by stronger ones. (WCHCD Collection)

Below: The Austin FX4 on display on Carbodies' stand at the 1959 Commercial Motor Exhibition. (Ivar Hellberg)

than cutting edge and owed little to Austin's private cars. It was a vehicle of its time, though nobody then would have believed that it would remain in service for almost half a century! At last, though (and at the recommendation of the PCO), it had four doors. Mechanically it was up to date, with suspension, axles and steering taken from current Austin models, along with hydraulic brakes specially adapted to dual circuit operation. Carried over from the FX3 were its reliable, long-lived 2.2-litre diesel engine, mated to a Borg-Warner DG150 automatic gearbox. Neither a manual gearbox nor a petrol engine were available. There was also a hire car version, the FL2 and a chassis-cab, which customers could send to various body builders, including hearse and van builders.

The FX4 was designed from the outset to be simple to maintain, with all its wings bolted on for ease of replacement. This, along with it being sold by a dedicated dealership with a reliable supply of spare parts made it the only real choice of the London cab trade. The only alternative was the Beardmore MkVII, which had limited servicing facilities and an obsolete appearance. The FX4 was introduced in 1958, but early production difficulties meant that it wouldn't be available in any real numbers until 1960.

The Minicab Threat

After the austerity of the post-war years, Britain's economy was finally starting to grow. People began to have more money in their pockets than they had ever done and wanted to go out and enjoy themselves. The number of cabs and cab drivers in London hadn't grown to meet public demand and in 1961, a small number of companies decided to offer an alternative to the taxi, in the form of small saloon cars hired through an office and controlled by radio. They were known as 'minicabs'. Though the public generally were pleased to see them, the illegal activities of some of the first companies' drivers caused great disruption and distress to the London cab trade. It also put the future of the purpose-built London taxi in doubt and delayed the development of three new cab models.

One of the original minicab companies was Welbeck Motors, which operated a fleet of red Renault Dauphines and it was this firm that achieved notoriety. Minicab drivers were not (and still are not) allowed to pick up off the streets or rank up in the same way a taxi driver can, so Welbeck's owner, Michael Gotla told his drivers that if they were approached in the street by a potential passenger, they were to make a booking via the car's two-way radio and a second car would be dispatched to collect the passenger. However, many of Welbeck's drivers simply broke the law and took the passenger themselves. The cab trade was in uproar over this blatant law-breaking and demanded that minicabs be banned. Instead, though, the government decided to see if purpose-built taxis were really necessary. They set up The Hackney Carriage Advisory Committee to examine the value of the Conditions of Fitness and decide whether ordinary saloon cars would do the job equally well in London, as they had been doing in cities around the world. It was not until mid-1962 that the Committee delivered its report, which recommended that the Conditions of Fitness

One of Welbeck Motors' Renault Dauphine minicabs, hemmed in by an FX3. (Stanley Roth Collection)

be retained, albeit with some detail changes, such as removing the requirement for cabs to have a separate chassis.

The Winchester

One of the new taxi models delayed by the Hackney Carriage Advisory Committee's deliberations was the Winchester, which had been started in 1960 as a competitor for the FX4 by the cab drivers' trade body, the Owner Drivers Society (ODA). The ODA ran its own taxi insurance scheme, Westminster Insurance and originally the cab was to be called the Westminster, but the name was already registered by Austin, so the ODA chose Winchester instead. It was the first London taxi to have a body made from fibreglass, built by James Whitson of West London. This was chosen because it was the cheapest option for the company's limited resources. Nor would it be prone to the body rust that was already affecting the FX4.

The Winchester was finally introduced in 1962. Sadly, it was very uncomfortable to drive and its Perkins 4.99 diesel engine made it very noisy. Just three were understood to have been sold. The Series II of 1964 had the option of a Ford Cortina petrol engine, which was quieter but only

The Beardmore MkVIII was a poor attempt by the company to produce a more up-to-date model. The PCO dismissed it out of hand. (Stanley Roth Collection)

The Series I Winchester was only available in two-tone grey. Just three are known to have been built. Subsequent versions were painted black. (Author's Collection)

about twelve were sold. The Series III of 1967, which had Ford Transit axles, engine and gearbox did little better with fourteen sold; overall, the Winchester proved a commercial failure by the time the Series III was dropped in 1967. The FX4 was so firmly established as the trade's vehicle of choice and its build quality, though somewhat poor at first, was being improved steadily.

The Beardmore MkVIII

The second new cab to be affected by the Conditions of Fitness review was the Beardmore MkVIII, but this was an ugly vehicle and Beardmore's finances were in such poor shape that they could afford to do no better. A second design for the MkVIII was mocked up by Weymann at Addlestone, but it too was scrapped. The introduction of a 4-door version of the MkVII was held up by a lengthy strike at Weymann's. The factory was closed after the strike and the company was absorbed by Metropolitan-Cammell, forming Metropolitan-Cammell-Weymann (MCW). The

From 1956, MkVII Beardmore bodies were built by Weymann in Surrey. Most were three-door models, but the last model, like this example, had four doors. (Author)

last Beardmores were built by MCW in Birmingham and the final example was sold in 1967.

The Mk2 Birch

John Birch thoroughly disliked the FX4 and in 1959 attempted to develop another new cab of his own, which was based on the Standard Atlas van. Its development was also delayed by the review of the Conditions of Fitness. When it was ready for inspection, the Home Office declared its steering and large front overhang potentially unsafe and refused to approve it. John Birch scrapped it and left the taxi business altogether.

Improvements for the FX4

The original automatic gearbox fitted to the FX4 proved unsuitable and it was replaced by the Borg-Warner BW35 automatic transmission. A

Mann & Overton's advert in The Steering Wheel *cab trade magazine shows the prices for the revised, 1968 model, though the illustration is of the original type. (Author's Collection)*

The 'New Shape" Austin FX4. As well as the external changes to the indicators and the incorporation of the sidelights into the headlamp fittings, the interior was revised, with a far better heater for the passengers and better legroom for the driver. Soundproofing was also added under the bonnet. (WCHCD Collection)

manual gearbox was offered from 1961 and a petrol engine became available from 1962.

In 1966, Mann & Overton started planning a replacement for the FX4 and asked Carbodies to quote for a new body. However, they felt that the price they were given was far too high and decided to have Carbodies upgrade the original model, which involved fitting a revised interior in black. The driver's compartment was redesigned to give more legroom. New taillights, from the Austin 1100 MkII were fitted, along with indicators fitted to the front wings. The darkened glass in the rear window was also changed to clear glass and for the first time, an inside rear-view mirror was allowed. The PCO insisted

The Metrocab prototype was built to the London General's brief for a smaller, lighter, more economical cab than the Austin FX4. Its fibreglass body, though light in weight, meant that The General would have to retrain all its body repair staff, which it wasn't prepared to do and so they pulled out of the project. (Author)

that this was fitted on the top of the dashboard, to prevent cab drivers from being tempted to use it to stare at the legs of a young woman passengers, particularly if that passenger was wearing a mini-skirt! The revised model became known unofficially in the trade as the "New Shape" FX4.

The Metrocab Prototype

In the late 1960s, challenger to the FX4, the Metrocab appeared. Its maker, Metropolitan-Cammell-Weymann, released two prototypes in 1968 and the was built in cooperation with the London General Cab Company in Brixton. They had a fibreglass bodies, to reduce weight and keep running and repair costs down and up-to-date styling to bring the design of the purpose-built taxi into the modern era. The were powered by a Perkins 4.108 diesel engine and had Ford Transit axles and suspension. The first example was run for two years by the London General Cab Company, on whose approval the project depended. However, the London General decided against investing in the Metrocab and the project was abandoned.

Winchester Series IV

The Winchester Series IV of 1968 was an altogether better vehicle than its predecessors. It also had a fibreglass body, and although the interior was basic, the cab had a completely modern appearance. It used an all-new chassis built by Keewest Engineering in Botley, Hants, Ford Transit axles and the option of either a 1,600cc Ford Cortina petrol or Perkins 4.108 diesel engine. It was introduced in 1968.

Its makers had not set up any dedicated service facilities outside of their own showroom in Chelsea and the small garages that were the backbone of the London cab trade would not repair them. Barely more than 30 were sold by the time it went out of production in 1971.

The Winchester Series 4 was a more attractive cab than the previous models, but the small scale of the manufacturers and the lack of widespread servicing facilities detracted buyers. (Author)

The revised model of Austin FX4 carried taillights sourced from BMC's MkII 1100/1330 range. A clear back window replaced the old darkened "purdah" glass that had been a carryover from the privacy expected by some passengers in older London cabs. (Author)

The FX4 - a Monopoly by Default

The last Beardmore MkVIIs disappeared from the streets as spares began to run out. Only the Series 4 Winchester, representing less than one per cent of the cabs licensed in London remained and the Metrocab project was abandoned. The Austin FX4 and Mann & Overton had been handed a complete monopoly, which would continue for a decade and a half.

Chapter 4

The Dominance of the Austin FX4

When the Austin FX4 first appeared, its top speed of 50mph was adequate in town, though its acceleration was rather sluggish compared to some of the new cars around. When the elevated section of the M4 motorway opened in 1965, cab drivers began using it as a fast route to Heathrow Airport, but the FX4's low top speed became a hindrance in fast motorway traffic. British Leyland, formed in 1968, developed a new

The 2.5 litre FX4 differed little visually from the previous 2.2 litre model, on which the aluminium sill trims appeared in 1970. The 'Rimbellisher' chrome wheel trims were an optional extra, as were mudflaps. (Author)

2.5 litre version of the Austin diesel engine, which was fitted to the FX4 in 1971. This improved its acceleration and put its top speed up to 70mph. Runs to Heathrow Airport along the M4 were now less stressful.

By the beginning of the 1970s, the FX4 was the only vehicle in which the Austin 2.2 litre petrol engine was offered. With sales of the petrol model at a standstill, Austin halted production of the engine. From 1974, new European vehicle safety regulations came into force. These required vehicles to be crash tested. The FX4 was suitably modified, with a crash link in the steering, a padded steering wheel boss and burst-proof door locks with push-button door handles. It passed the test and the model with the modifications appeared in late 1973.

A 1977 brochure for the FX4. Note the push-button door handles and opening quarterlights, which were introduced in 1973 and the plastic overriders, which were fitted from 1977. (Author's collection)

A New Owner for Carbodies

The future of the FX4 was put in jeopardy in around 1972, because the BSA Group, which had owned Carbodies since 1954 was heading for collapse. In 1973, BSA's motorcycle companies and the few companies that remained within the BSA group, including Carbodies were sold to Manganese Bronze Holdings Plc (MBH), which owned BSA's rival British motorcycle maker, Associated Motorcycles Ltd. The motorcycle companies were combined into one group, Norton-Villiers-Triumph (NVT). MBH was keen to continue making the FX4, which at this time was Carbodies' principal product. Thus the future of the FX4 and of its maker was secured.

The Lucas Electric Taxi

In 1975, Lucas Industries Ltd, the supplier of automotive electric equipment to the British Motor Industry introduced a prototype electric London taxi. It was one of three types of experimental electric vehicle built by the company, the others being a midibus and a conversion of the Bedford CF van. It was designed by Ogle Associates and at 140.5in (3,570mm), it was 40in (1,010mm) shorter than the Austin FX4. Two examples were built, with a fibreglass body reinforced by a steel frame, mounted on a steel perimeter chassis. The 50bhp motor was mounted transversely at the front

One of the two Lucas electric taxis built. It was a metre shorter than the Austin FX4. (WCHCD Archive)

and drove the front wheels. The lead/acid batteries gave a range of around 70-80 miles (112-128km) at a maximum speed of 50mph (88kph). The range was its major shortcoming, as a London taxi might at least double that daily mileage and there were no public charging points available. As an experimental vehicle it attracted interest, but its limited range made it impractical and the experiment was discontinued.

The FX5

Carbodies' Managing Director, Bill Lucas felt that Mann & Overton could sell more taxis than they were doing. This was critical for Carbodies, because the work they had been doing throughout the post-war period, which included making Ford Zephyr convertibles and Triumph 2000 and Humber estate car bodies, had all but disappeared and the taxi was their major product. In about 1976, in an attempt to break free from the arrangement with Mann & Overton, Lucas began the development of a Carbodies cab, which he called the FX5. This had an entirely new chassis and a new pressed steel body of completely modern appearance. A scale model was made and it received a warm welcome from the trade.

The scale model of the FX5 that was presented to the cab trade. (Author's Collection/ Barney Sharratt)

The Silver Jubilee FX4

The London cab trade wanted to honour HM Queen Elizabeth II on the occasion of her Silver Jubilee in 1975. The then Prince of Wales invited a delegation of cab trade representatives to Buckingham Palace and the London General Cab Company brought along several vehicles from their museum. Carbodies' contribution was a special FX4 in silver, with the Jubilee logo hand painted on the doors. The Prince drove it around the palace courtyard, before borrowing it for his official duties for the rest of the day!

New Purchase Options for the FX4

The unemployment created by the industrial unrest of the 1970s drove an increasing number of men to sign on to the Knowledge of London. The number of cab drivers in London rose from 9,586 in 1971 to 12,267 in 1979 and over the same period, the number of cabs licensed annually rose from 13,819 to 17,076. A new Consumer Credit Act made it far easier for cab

HRH the Prince of Wales drove the Jubilee FX4 in the courtyard of Buckingham Palace. (LEVC)

By the end of the 1970s, the number of owner-driven cabs had risen considerably. This 1981 Austin FX4 is one of many that had different colour paint and vinyl roofs. (LEVC)

drivers to buy new vehicles. Both Mann & Overton and Carbodies were happy with this, as it boosted sales. Carbodies also knew that owner-drivers used their cabs as family cars as well, so thought they would also like to have them with some additional comforts and in different colours. New options such as sunshine roofs and vinyl roofs and several new colours, including midnight blue and champagne beige were added to the original options of carmine red and white and some other, less successful options of tan, green and aconite (a bright purple) that had been offered during the 1970s. The new colours sold well and besides increasing profits for both Carbodies and Mann & Overton, brightened up London's streets in the process. Now, from around 1980, the "black cab" could be seen in blue, red, white, green or beige.

Chapter 5

The Creation of LTI and the Introduction of MCW's Metrocab

At the end of the 1970s, constant industrial disputes, excessive overheads and the poor quality of its cars brought Austin's owner, British Leyland, to the brink of collapse. To try and save the company, the government part-nationalised it and brought in industrialist Michael Edwardes to bring it back to profitability.

One of the first FX4s made under Carbodies own name is parked for a publicity shot by Edinburgh Castle. The badge on the grille was not the one chosen for production. (LEVC)

An FX4R prototype, parked in the centre of Coventry, near Holy Trinity Church and the statue of Lady Godiva. Note the single blister on the front of the bonnet, included to accommodate the bulkier power steering box. Production FX4Rs would have a blister on either side, as the cab was planned for export as well as home sales. (LEVC)

The new European Whole Vehicle Type Approval requirement was on the horizon for all British-made vehicles and BL, as Edwardes had renamed British Leyland, showed no interest in making sure the FX4 met them. The taxi would be forced out of production if it didn't comply, so in early 1982, Carbodies negotiated with BL to buy the intellectual rights to the FX4, which enabled Carbodies to acquire type approval for it in their own name. From mid-1982 it was badged as the Carbodies FX4. However, in acquiring the rights to the vehicle, Carbodies lost the subsidy that Austin provided and this resulted in an increase in price, from around £7,000 to over £8,000.

The Carbodies FX4R

BL also sold off the taxi's Austin diesel engine to an Indian manufacturer because it no longer complied with European emissions standards. The only viable replacement for the FX4 was the 2.2 litre Land Rover diesel, which was installed in a new model, the FX4R, along with the option of a 3-speed automatic or a 5-speed manual gearbox. It was introduced in late 1982 and had, for the first time in a London taxi, power steering and full servo brakes. It was available in three trim options: the Fleetline (FL), the Highline (HL) and the Highline Special (HLS). The development costs meant an increase in prices, to £8,869 for an FL manual and £10,071 for an HLS automatic with power steering. Although the quietness of the Land Rover diesel and the power steering were appreciated, the fuel consumption and acceleration were poor and the engine and the manual gearbox proved unreliable. Sales dropped considerably as a consequence at a time when Carbodies needed to increase their income.

The CR6

The FX5 project was scrapped because it would have been too expensive to build, but a new taxi was still needed and development of another design, based on a Range Rover body was begun. This was called the CR6 – C for City, R for Rover and 6 to follow the '5' of FX5 – and was scheduled to replace the FX4 within about three years. However, in June 1980, the Department of Transport ran a seminar to address the transport needs of disabled people. One of the biggest demands from delegates in wheelchairs was that taxis should be more accessible to them. Carbodies duly adapted the CR6 prototype to do so and built a second prototype, with wheelchair accessibility built in from the start. The Department of Transport bought both and put them on trial outside London to assess their suitability as wheelchair accessible vehicles. The trials showed that the cabs needed many modifications, including a higher roof, but by now the cost had grown to an extremely high level and Carbodies announced in January 1986 that they were scrapping the CR6. Their press release stressed the importance of the FX4's traditional shape, saying it was recognised by people the world over. The reality was that they simply had neither the people nor the money to bring the CR6 to production. Continuing with the FX4 was their only option.

The FX4Q

With the FX4R failing to sell in sufficient numbers, Carbodies decided to offer rebuilt cabs to the trade. They bought in decommissioned cabs, discarded the bodies, overhauled the suspension and brakes, fitted a completely new body and an Indian made Austin diesel engine. Because the cab was built on an existing chassis, the UK licensing authorities gave each cab a new, non-age-related registration number, prefixed by the letter

The first CR6 prototype. Its Range Rover origins are clear to see. (Stanley Roth Collection)

Q. They were sold by a London taxi proprietor, E. A. Crouch of Hackney. Mann & Overton, were, unsurprisingly furious that Carbodies had made such a decision.

The Formation of London Taxis International

In 1984, Mann & Overton's owner Lloyds Bowmaker, decided to put the dealership up for sale. MBH moved quickly to buy both the dealership and its finance house and from this acquisition, formed a new organisation, London Taxis International, with three divisions: LTI Carbodies to make the cabs, LTI Mann & Overton to sell them and London Taxi Finance (LTF) to fund the sales. Now design, development and sales of the cab were all brought in-house.

The FX4Q looked no different from the Austin FX4. This preserved example has had the original rubber overriders replaced with older-type chrome plated steel ones. (Author)

The FX4S

The replacement for the FX4R, the FX4S was introduced in November 1985 and was powered by Land Rover's new 2.5-litre engine. It was the first model of cab to carry LTI badges (though its maker was officially Carbodies). It differed in other details from previous FX4s in having rocker switches on the dashboard, new steering column controls for the indicators and lights, new black bumpers and silver wheels. It performed far better than the FX4R and, once some teething troubles had been sorted out, sold much better than the FX4R.

LTI's publicity shot of the FX4S. Note the black rolled steel bumpers and the silver wheels, which distinguish the FX4S from previous FX4 models. (LEVC)

The London Coach and London Sterling

Attempts to sell London taxis to the USA had always failed, largely because the cab was far more expensive to buy than the domestic sedans used by the cab trade there. In 1984, Grant Lockhart did a deal with American specialist vehicle manufacturer D. F. Landers to assemble the FX4 in the USA. The Land Rover engine would not comply with US federal exhaust emission regulations, so a 2.3 litre Ford petrol engine was supplied for the cab. Two models were offered, the London Coach, which was a luxury taxi version and the London Sterling, which was a limousine version. This came with a huge range of optional extras. Although sales started well, a change in the exchange rate made the vehicles far too expensive and the contract was cancelled after just fifty of the first two hundred vehicles had been delivered.

The brochure for the American model London Coach taxi and London Sterling limousine shows many detail differences between it and the donor FX4S. The bumpers were heavy-duty types required by US federal law. The UK-style taxi roof sign would not be fitted. (Author's Collection)

The Metrocab

In the mid-1980s, Metro-Cammell-Weymann revisited the Metrocab project. They brought in engineers Geoff Chater from Carbodies and Bob Parsons from Chrysler UK to design a new cab from scratch. Like the previous effort, it was called the Metrocab. It had a 5-seater fibreglass body with a totally modern shape. Power was by a 4-cylinder Ford Transit diesel engine, coupled to a Ford 4-speed automatic transmission. Most importantly, it was the first London taxi purpose-built to carry a passenger in a wheelchair. This was essential because wheelchair accessibility would be mandatory on all new London taxis by January 1 1989. It was launched in December 1986 and it was the first real competitor the FX4 had ever had. Though welcomed at first, a shortage of service and repair facilities and, later, troubles with the gearbox, gave it a bad reputation and sales stalled.

Carbodies' subsidiary company, Carbodies Sales & Services Ltd developed a wheelchair conversion for the FX4. Here the engineer responsible for the work, Roger Ponticelli pushes a passenger in a wheelchair into the cab. Note the passenger door, which is hinged on the B-pillar. (Craig Ponticelli)

Above: MCW's Metrocab, pictured with a Metrobus. (Steve Tillyer)

Below: A Royal Burgundy FX4S-Plus ranks up at London City Airport. (Author)

The FX4S-Plus

Despite the arrival of the Metrocab, LTI remained dominant in the purpose-built taxi market, but they were by no means complacent and knew they had to develop a new model, not only to meet the demands of the London trade, but to expand into provincial and export markets. As the company was short of cash, the new model would have to be developed step by step. The first step was to make the FX4 more comfortable, by revamping the entire interior, with a new moulded dashboard and a smarter passenger compartment that sat 5 people. This new interior was used in the next model, which was named the FX4S-Plus. Mechanically it was almost the same as the FX4S, but with GKN Literide composite rear springs and telescopic rear shock absorbers. It was launched in September 1987 at the Taxi Driver of the Year Show in London's Battersea Park to a great reception. The top of the range HLS automatic sold for £13,678.45. An aftermarket wheelchair conversion was offered on the cab, supplied by Carbodies' subsidiary company, Carbodies Sales & Services Ltd for £998.

One of the last FX4S-Plus cabs built. This example has had its original grille replaced by a Fairway item. (Author/Barney Sharratt)

Chapter 6

The Fairway, More Metrocabs and the Asquith

The Metrocab received a mixed reception from the London cab trade. Whilst it was welcomed as a competitor for the FX4, the problems with the gearbox, plus the fact that several components were fragile, created justifiable criticism. The dealers, Metro Sales & Service Ltd were powerless to resolve the problems, as The Laird Group, owners of Metro Cammell Weymann Ltd, were in trouble and gave the Metrocab division few, if any

Hooper's promotional picture of their first Metrocabs. The wheel trims were of a revised design; the original type were notorious for working loose and rolling away into the traffic! (Taxi Newspaper)

resources to fix the cab's problems. Even if the Metrocab had been more reliable and there were better service facilities available, drivers encountered some degree of resistance by the public to hail it, because it looked so unlike their impression of a London taxi. Whilst the press release that LTI sent out to announce scrapping of the CR6 may have seemed like a poor excuse for the new model's failure, it was indeed true that the FX4 had been around for so long that for younger Londoners it was the only taxi they had ever known and its shape was totally recognisable for what it was.

MCW's owners, the Laird Group went bust and the Metrocab was sold to Reliant, who had been making the bodies for it. They had hopes for developing the vehicle and the business further, but in 1990 the holding company that owned Reliant went under in the property crash that immediately preceded the recession of the early 1990s. Metrocab was sold to Hooper & Company (Coachbuilders) Ltd, who invested heavily in the vehicle, adding disc brakes in 1992 and a 6-seater version in 1994.

The Fairway

LTI's next step in developing a new model was to source a new engine and dedicated gearboxes. This was found in the Japanese Nissan TD27, a 4-cylinder diesel, along with matching 4-speed automatic and 5-speed manual gearboxes. Though it was a hard decision in one way to fit Japanese power into something so typically British, the engine and transmissions were of such good quality they could not be turned down.

The engine was fitted into a new model, the Fairway, which was launched in February 1989. It was LTI's first wheelchair accessible model and it complied with new laws requiring wheelchair accessibility that came into force on January 1 1989. The FX4S-Plus's interior was carried over with modifications that included a lift-up rear seat to allow a wheelchair to be manoeuvred into place. It was available in three trim options; the basic Bronze model, the Silver, which came with carpeting all round, a vinyl roof

Above: one of the first Fairways, from 1989. This is the Gold model, with the standard sun roof, vinyl roof and chrome side strips. The colour is midnight blue, which was a very popular option to the standard black. (Author)

Below: from the early 1990s, London's cabs were permitted to carry all-over advertisements, known as liveries. The cabs' owners and were paid a fixed price for a set period. The liveries were changed whenever the contract with the advertiser expired. The Guinnes livery carried by this 1990 Fairway is particularly striking. (Author's Collection)

and a sliding sunroof and the Gold, which had heavy-duty carpeting in the passenger compartment and wood finish door and window cappings. It was met with great praise for its performance and relative silence and it sold extremely well. Unsurprisingly, it was noticeably more expensive that the S-Plus, at £16,749.75 for the top model, the Gold automatic.

The Fairway Driver

LTI's third step towards a new model arrived in February 1992, with the addition of disc brakes and new double-wishbone front suspension with telescopic shock absorbers to the Fairway. Facilities for disabled passengers were improved with the addition of a slot-in low step and an adaptation of the nearside tip-up seat, which enabled it to swing out to assist the less mobile to climb into the cab. The model was named the Fairway Driver. It came in just one trim option and, like the original Fairway, the choice of automatic or manual transmissions. The automatic model, by far the most popular in London sold for £21,618.

This unused LTI publicity shot of the Fairway Driver shows the distinctive domed wheel covers designed to fit over the deep-dished wheels that were fitted to cover the new brakes. (LEVC)

Above: this early Fairway Driver carries a United Airlines livery. Note the small wheelchair logos on either side of the roof sign glass. (Author's Collection)

Below: wheelchair accessibility for the Fairway (and also the Metrocab) was gained by the use of these removable ramps, which were stowed in the boot when not in use. (LEVC Archive)

The Asquith

At the beginning of the 1980s, Crispin Reed and Bruce West ran a business in Essex making reproduction furniture. The 1928 Austin 12 van they used for deliveries gave them great publicity, but it was unreliable, so they fitted a Ford Transit chassis with a vintage-style van body. It attracted a lot of attention, so they decided to make more and they built up a business, producing around one hundred vehicles a year, selling them in the UK and around the world.

When a London cab driver visited the works, he remarked that the vans looked like pre-war cabs, which gave Reed the idea to make a taxi. The result was a cab in the style of a pre-war cab, but with modern mechanical components, 4 doors, 5 seats and full wheelchair accessibility. The body

One of the very few Asquith retro-style cabs made. Though well-appointed, it was expensive. (Author)

was of fibreglass, the engine and automatic gearbox were the same Ford units used in the Metrocab and the rear axle and front suspension came from the Vauxhall Frontera. It was launched in April 1994, with a base price of £29,950, which was at least £8,500 more than a Fairway Driver. The high price and the fact that it was made and sold by a company with no history in the cab trade and thus no understanding of the trade's requirements, deterred potential buyers. So, sadly did its unique selling point, its retro design. Serious reliability issues and a failure to deliver spares in good time also hit sales and, in the end, only about a dozen were sold. A mock-up of a new model, with a modern body was displayed at the 1996 London Motor Fair, but financial troubles within the company forced them into liquidation in 1997. The existing cab went out of production and plans for the new model was abandoned.

New Metrocab Models

Hooper produced two more models of Metrocab, the restyled Series II in late 1995 and the upgraded Series III, with electric windows all round in November 1997. Both retained the Ford Transit diesel engine.

A digitally created image of the proposed modern-style Asquith cab. (Stanley Roth Collection)

Above: three TX1s leaving Paddington Station. Silver was the second most popular colour choice after black. (Author)

Below: a Metrocab Series II, photographed in London's Oxford Circus. At one point, the Series II could be ordered in any colour the buyer chose. (Author)

This Fairway taxi was originally an FL2 limousine, which was retrofitted by Tickford's with a petrol engine, which in turn was converted to run on compressed natural gas, drawn from the domestic mains supply. It was then rebuilt as a taxi and licensed for use in London. (Stanley Roth)

The LTI TX1

Finally the Fairway's Nissan engine and new suspension and brakes were incorporated into a new model, the TX1. In accordance with LTI's market research, the cab's main stylist, Wayne Burgess, took his styling cues from the FX4. The renowned industrial designer Sir Kenneth Grange was invited to produce some designs, but as these did not take into consideration the required retro look, they were not taken up.

The TX1 was launched at the London Motor Show in October 1997. The public identified it as a cab immediately it came out, so similar did it appear to the old model. It was free of the body rattles and leaks endemic in the FX4 and its big windscreen, combined with more driver space offered far better visibility and comfort. The TX1 broke all sales records for London cabs and by June 1999, LTI announced the sale of its 5,000th example.

Gas Fuelled Taxis

From the late 1990s there were several trials of London cabs fitted with engines running on either liquid propane gas (LPG) or liquefied natural gas (LNG). British Gas ran a Carbodies FL2 converted to LNG by

Hooper Metrocab's Sales Director, Steve Ferris delivers an LPG-fuelled Series III Metrocab to His Royal Highness the Duke of Edinburgh. It was the third of three Metrocabs that he ran, for his royal duties in London. (Taxi Newspaper)

Tickford's, which was subsequently converted to a taxi and was licensed in London for several years.

LTI fitted three Fairways with Iveco spark ignition engines converted to gas operation in late 1997 and later, ran four TX1s with Ford bi-fuel engines running on LPG. A Fairway fitted with a Rover K-Series 4-cylinder petrol engine converted to gas by the Ecological Engine Company was offered by LTI dealers KPM (UK) Plc in the late 1990s. The London Central Cab company offered the fitting of the 2.3 Ford DOHC petrol engine, adapted to run on gas in both LTI cabs and in particular the Metrocab, for just over £12,000. This engine ran without any reported trouble. None of these experiments established liquefied gas as a viable fuel for London taxis, partly because the life of the spark ignition engines was shorter than that of a contemporary diesel, so the whole life cost was greater than that of a diesel cab.

Chapter 7

The LTI TX-Series and the LEVC TX

The biggest single factor affecting the London taxi during the 21st century has been exhaust emissions and the need to clean up the capital's air. This came from two sources; the European Union and Transport for London (TfL), through The Greater London Authority. The EU's directives have focused on exhaust emission standards for all vehicles, but TfL went much further in demanding that all new London taxis be zero-emission capable from 2018.

The LTI TXII

The European Union's Euro 3 standard for motor vehicle exhaust emissions came into force on January 1 2001. The Fairway's Nissan TD27 engine could not be adapted to comply with them and as Nissan had no suitable replacement, LTI had to look elsewhere. Negotiations with Isuzu to use their diesel engine collapsed with a year to go before the new regulations came into force and LTI were in a tight spot. Most engine makers wanted at least two years' development time, except Ford, which provided the Duratorq 2.4 litre turbodiesel engine. As Ford did not have an automatic transmission compatible with this engine, the Nissan's transmission was adapted to fit. The cab was launched in January 2002. Its lack of development time proved disastrous, as the Ford engine was unreliable. The problems were largely rectified but the drop in sales hurt LTI.

Above: December 6 2001 saw the first TXII leave LTI's production line at Holyhead Road, Coventry. (LTI)

Below: To celebrate the Golden Jubilee of HM Queen Elizabeth II, fifty cabs, mostly TXIIs were painted gold and carried special logos. LTI held a launch in Coventry, by the Cathedral. Leaning on the window is LTI's then CEO, Peter Shillcock. (LTI)

The Metrocab TTT and the beginning of the end for the Company

The Ford diesel engine that Metrocab had been using was phased out, as it would not meet the Euro 3 exhaust emission standards. However, rather than buy the Ford Duratorq, as LTI had done, Metrocab opted for Toyota's 2.4-litre turbodiesel. The new model in which it was fitted was named the TTT and it appeared in 2001. It was generally recognised as the finest Metrocab model. However, attempts by the company to build a much bigger cab that would comply with expected but as yet unclear disability regulations drained the company of resources. The firm ceased production and was eventually sold to Malaysian-based company KamKorp.

The LTI TX4

The EU's Euro 4 exhaust emission standard was scheduled to come into force on January 1 2006. To comply with this, LTI developed the TX4, so named because its VM turbodiesel engine complied with Euro 4; there would be no TX3 model. Along with the engine came dedicated transmissions, sourced from Chrysler. ABS brakes, which had been made a requirement of the Conditions of Fitness, were standard. The TX4 was distinguished from the TXII by a new, full height grille, restyled front bumper and new taillights. Four models were offered: the entry-level Driver, Bronze, Silver and Gold.

Green Power Experiments

In April 2003, Manganese Bronze Plc signed an agreement with Azure Dynamics of Canada to develop a hybrid electric motive power system for use in a cab. Azure fitted a TXII with their powertrain in June 2003, but this project was abandoned. Frazer-Nash, once a famous British sports car company but in the early 21st century a subsidiary of Metrocab's owner, KamKorp fitted a hybrid powerplant into a restyled Metrocab in early

Above: Based on the previous Series III model, the Metrocab TTT was identifiable by the grille badge. (Author)

Below: The TX4 would be the last ever diesel-powered London taxi made by LTI. The front cab is an LTI version and behind is the later, London Taxi Company version, identified by the circular grille badge. (Author)

2008, but nothing more was heard of it. Metrocab was sold to the Malaysian company KamKorp and their subsidiary Frazer-Nash fitted a hybrid powerplant into a restyled Metrocab in early 2008, but the project was not followed through.

LTI and Lotus Engineering developed a TX4 to run on hydrogen fuel cell power. An example was demonstrated at the Goodwood Festival of Speed in 2012 and several cabs hydrogen fuel cell cabs appeared in the closing ceremony of the London 2012 Olympic Games. However, no hydrogen fuel cell taxis were produced for sale.

The Mercedes-Benz Vito

Though Metrocab had ceased production, LTI would not have the market to itself for long. A new arrival was a taxi based on the Mercedes-Benz Vito Traveliner MPV. The Traveliner had proven itself in cab work worldwide, but its turning circle disqualified it from being type-approved for London.

This hydrogen fuel cell powered TX4 was developed in conjunction with Lotus Engineering Ltd. It is seen here beginning a demonstration run at the Goodwood Festival of Speed in 2012. (LTI)

Above: Rather than undertake to re-engineer the front-wheel steering, Penso, the company that converted the Vito into a taxi, chose to design and install rear wheel steering. (Sandie Goodwin/Taxi Globe)

Below: The Mercedes-Benz Vito secured a place in the London taxi trade by being an up-market vehicle. Because it didn't resemble a traditional London taxi, the Vito taxi could be specified with distinctive red "taxi" side flashes. (Author)

The problem of meeting the 7.6m turning circle requirement was solved by fitting part-time rear-wheel steering, which was activated at speeds below 5mph. Sliding doors were standard on the Traveliner, but a new rule in the Conditions of Fitness required them to be power-assisted. Electrically operated low steps were also fitted, extending and retracting as required. The Vito Taxi was type approved on June 26 2008 and launched immediately after. It was a full six-seater with mandatory wheelchair accessibility, powered by a 2.15 litre four-cylinder turbocharged diesel engine, coupled to a full automatic transmission with Tiptronic control. It had independent suspension and disc brakes all round with ABS and power-assisted steering.

The public were unsure whether the Vito was a genuine London taxi and often would let one pass by rather than hail it on the street. However, the Vito began winning back corporate contract work lost to private hire companies, which were using luxury saloon cars. A Euro 5 version of the Vito arrived in the spring of 2011, distinguished by new lights and bumpers.

The Creation of The London Taxi Company

LTI had begun to achieve some export success with the Fairway and the TX-series built on that with some success. However, their Coventry factory was aging and inefficient, so to both replace it and find lower production costs, LTI began looking for an overseas partner to establish a factory in a country where labour was cheap. This, LTI hoped, would provide a manufacturing base for export vehicles at lower cost and allow for expansion while a new UK factory was sought. In September 2006, Geely Automotive of Shanghai, China acquired 20 per cent of MBH and began building a new factory in Shanghai, to build cabs for the Chinese and other overseas markets and to make complete CKD kits for assembly in Coventry. The company was renamed The London Taxi Company (LTC), which embraced both manufacture and sales and after over a century of service to the cab trade, the trading name of Mann & Overton was dropped. In late 2010 the first models for the UK market carrying the LTC name, the Style and the Elegance model were announced.

Geely Acquires LTC

Production of the TX4 was halted in 2011 when a batch of new steering boxes that were made in China proved faulty. This stopped the company's cash flow in its tracks and in October 2012, Manganese Bronze Holdings Plc was forced into administration. The future of the taxi looked to be doomed, as although the Mercedes Vito was readily available, sales did not rise to take up what LTC had lost. Three months later, a deal was done whereby Geely bought the remainder of MBH. Geely restarted taxi production in September 2013.

Cleaner Air for London

In October 2010, London's newly elected mayor, Boris Johnson published a document entitled Delivering London's Energy Future. Johnson pledged to make London, "the greenest city in the world" by 2025. Along with other diesel vehicles, taxis were targeted. By 2011, cabs over 15 years old would not be licensed, unless they were powered by cleaner fuels such as LPG or CNG. Transport for London, the licensing authority for London's cab trade since 2000 announced that from 2018, all newly licensed London taxis would have to be zero emissions-capable.

The Nissan NV200 London Taxi

In New York City in 2007, the city officials brought together interested parties to discuss what would best be incorporated in a future taxi for the city. This led to a "Taxi of Tomorrow" competition, the winner of which was announced on May 3, 2011 and was a design by Nissan North America, Inc based on the NV200 Vanette taxi already in use in Tokyo.

In August 2012 Nissan unveiled a London version of the NV200, with new front suspension, designed by UK engineering consultancy Vectayn Ltd to accommodate the 7.62m turning circle. Engine options included a 1.5-litre, four-cylinder eight-valve turbodiesel engine, coupled to a 5-speed or a 6-speed manual, and later a petrol engine. The launch was to be rounded off with an all-electric model sometime in early 2014, but no model entered production.

The Metrocab REEV

In January 2014, Metrocab, by this time in the ownership of Malaysian group KamKorp, announced an all-new, purpose-built Range Extended Electric taxi. It seated 6 passengers or three able-bodied passengers and two passengers in wheelchairs. Two prototypes were built and demonstrated, but by 2018, the development company, Frazer Nash had over

Metrocab, under the ownership of the Malaysian company KamKorp, developed two prototype electric London taxis, which were launched at City Hall. This is the second prototype. (Sandie Goodwin/Taxi Globe)

Above: the London Taxi Company first announced in January 2014 that they would be building an all-new electric London taxi. This is one of two the images they released to promote it. (LTC)

£1.5m of unpaid debts and the company was wound up. The new Metrocab never went into production.

The LEVC TX5/TXE

Transport for London, which had taken over the duties of the Public Carriage Office in 2000 announced that all new taxis licensed in London from 2018 had to be zero-emissions-capable. To meet this requirement, The London Taxi Company began work on a new electric taxi, initially named the TX5. A concept vehicle was announced in October 2015 at Lancaster House, London, coinciding with a visit to the UK by Chinese president Xi Jinping. Announced too was a new factory, to be built on a brownfield site at Ansty, Coventry.

The taxi prototype underwent a considerable amount of testing in extreme climates, including in the Arctic, using facilities belonging to Volvo, another of Geely's companies.

The production version of the electric taxi, renamed as the TX was unveiled on August 1 2017 and its order books were opened. The launch also announced a new company name, the London Taxi Corporation and a new trading name, the London Electric Vehicle Company, or LEVC.

The vehicle was built on a platform of aluminium panels, bonded together, to which composite body panels are fixed. Its drive motor is electric, powered by batteries mounted under the driver's compartment and luggage platform. The batteries can be recharged by a range-extender, a 3-cylinder Volvo petrol engine coupled to a generator, should they run low. Suspension and steering were sourced from Volvo models. The factory opened in 2017, manufacture of the cab began and it went on sale in January 2018. The claimed range of the vehicle was 64 miles running on the battery alone, or 318 miles using the range extender. By April 2020, LEVC announced they had sold 5,000 examples in London alone.

July 2017 marked the launch of both the TX electric taxi and the announcement of a change of name for the manufacturer, from The London Taxi Company to The London Electric Vehicle Company (LEVC) (Author)

In May 2023, LEVC announced a battery upgrade for new TX taxis, which promised an increased electric-only range of 78 miles and a total range, using the range extender, of 333 miles.

The Nissan Dynamo

The Nissan Dynamo taxi, based on the Nissan NV200 Evalia MPV was introduced in October 2019. It was a pure battery electric vehicle, seating five passengers and with full wheelchair accessibility. The MPV version was used instead of the van, because the driver's compartment was better equipped. Though it sold well enough at the start, its production was brought a halt when Nissan discontinued the base model after more than twenty years' production. Dynamo Motors announced that it was seeking a new manufacturer with which to cooperate in bringing out a new taxi model, but filed for liquidation in November 2022.

This picture of a Nissan Dynamo taxi plugged into a charging point beside one of the few cabmen's shelters remaining in London represents a mixture of the traditional and the modern aspects of the London cab trade. (Dynamo Engineering)

Before its launch, LEVC's new electric taxi was known as the TX5, as can be seen in this picture.

Below: when the cab came to market, the "5" was dropped and it is now marketed as the TX. (LEVC)

Living with new Emissions Regulations

The TfL regulation requiring that all new London taxis had to be zero-emissions capable did not signal the immediate end of the internal-combustion engine cab. A small number of TX models have been fitted with gas-powered engines that do comply with the then current European regulations and an adaptation for the Mercedes-Benz Vito has brought it up to Euro 6, giving the older vehicles a longer life.

Conclusion

The "Black Cab" has been with us for over seventy years and the London cab trade itself has been around in one form or another for almost four centuries. Both the trade and the cab manufacturers have faced many challenges, technical, administrative and legal and without doubt they will face more. Can the "Black cab", last much longer? As long as the public want a trusted, accountable taxi service and are willing to pay a fare that funds the maintnenace of the safety standards that are currently in place, there will be people who will provide it. And as long as there is at least one company prepared to make a vehicle that meets the requirements laid down for these unique vehicles, there will surely be a "black cab" of some description.

The Public Carriage Office

When in 1843 the Metropolitan Police was given responsibility for licensing London's cabs, it formed a dedicated branch, the Public Carriage Office, in order to carry out these duties. Its primary duty was to safeguard the travelling public by ensuring that all drivers acted responsibly and that cabs were properly maintained and built to meet a standard that ensured safety and convenience for the passengers. That responsibility remains with the current licensing regime.

The Metropolitan Police, including the PCO was originally under the control of the Home Office. In 1982, the duty of licensing cabs passed to the Department of Transport, although enforcement remained with the police, under Cab Enforcement Branch. In 2000, control of the Metropolitan Police, including the Public Carriage Office, was transferred to the newly formed Greater London Authority. This moved London's cab trade from national to local government control, although all the statute law (i. e. legislation passed by Parliament rather than by local authorities) governing the cab trade remained in place. In 2010 the GLA replaced the PCO with Taxis and Private Hire (TfL TPH), to include the minicab trade that had come under its own, PCO controlled licensing regime since 2000.

Under the PCO, taxis had to undergo a rigorous examination by their examiners (Carriage Officers, or CO's) in order to be licensed. Until the 1960s, CO's were serving police officers but now they are civilians. The original Conditions of Fitness set standards for cab construction that were in some circumstances higher than the national standards for motor vehicles. The inspection regime predated the MoT by half a century. To be licensed, a cab had to be overhauled and presented at one of the PCO's passing stations and if it met the standards required, the proprietor was issued with a licence for a calendar year and given a pair of licence plates, one to be fixed to the rear of the cab and another fixed inside the cab, in clear view of the passengers. The plates remained the property of the Metropolitan Police and had to be handed back when the full calendar year had expired, or before, if the full prescribed life of the cab had been reached. In the 1960s and 1970s this was ten years. It was extended during the 1980s but at the time of writing it is twelve years. The licence plates have no commercial value, unlike taxi licence plates issued by taxi licensing authorities outside London, which can be bought and sold.

The headquarters of the Public Carriage Office at Scotland Yard, London in the late Victorian era. Though a two-storey building, it acquired the nickname of "The Bungalow". (WCHCD Archive)

For years, there was no fee charged to pass a cab, but in the 1980s, a fee was introduced and has been in place ever since.

Cabs were, and still are liable for quarterly inspections. The COs undertook regular street patrols, checking for unroadworthy cabs. If they found one, they would issue an unfit notice, commonly known as a 'stop note'. The proprietor then had to fix whatever the problem was and present it to a passing station before the cab could be worked once more.

The PCO has occupied three premises during its control of the London cab trade, the first being a single building at Scotland Yard, adjacent to the Metropolitan Police's HQ in London's Westminster, known as "The Bungalow". The Metropolitan Police's duties grew considerably throughout the late nineteenth and early twentieth centuries and a new building was opened in 1927 in Lambeth Road, South London to accommodate

Completed in 1963, the Public Carriage Office's premises in Penton Street, Islington was typical of the architecture used for government buildings at the time. (Roy Ellis)

various administrative functions, such as lost property, The Receiver's Office (the department that handled external financial transactions), the police garage and the PCO. Here, facilities for approving new cabs and inspecting and licensing existing cabs were provided. Also new cabs were presented for their first licence and new types of cab or cabs with any new modifications were presented for Type Approval.

Originally, the PCO divided London into ten administrative districts, each with at least one Passing Station, where cabs were inspected and licensed. Following the move to Lambeth, the number of districts was reduced to four, though still with several Passing Stations in each. By the 1950s, there was just one Passing Station in each district. By then, the Lambeth Road premises were becoming overcrowded, so it was decided to move the departments into new premises of their own. In 1965 the PCO

Cabs undergoing inspection for relicensing at the PCO in Penton Street. The orange devices attached to the cabs' exhaust tailpipes are particulate filters, attached whilst the cabs were on the premises to keep the air in the building clean. (Author's Collection)

Each London taxi is licensed for a period of one calendar year and a plate is issued, showing the period from which the ilcence runs. Once the period has expired, the plate is returned to Transport for London adn is destroyed. (Author)

moved to new, purpose-built premises at Penton Street, Islington, where The Knowledge of London examinations and the licensing of cabs, cab proprietors and drivers were carried out and also where the Lost Property Office was housed. It remained the home of the PCO until 2010 when it was closed down.

Today, taxis are required to undergo two standard MoT tests per year, after which they are required to be examined at an approved centre to ensure they comply with the Conditions of Fitness. If the vehicle passes, a licence is granted for a full calendar year. The plate given to the proprietor carries the licence number, the registration number, the expiry date and the number of passengers the cab is permitted to carry. TfL TPH's offices are currently housed in a building named Palestra, in London's Blackfriars.

Further Reading

Bobbitt, Malcolm. Taxi! The Story if the London Taxicab. Veloce, 2002

The history of the London cab, in concise form, for the general enthusiast. P/b, b/w & colour. Out of Print

Farrell, Sean. Abstracts of Black Cab Lore. Amazon, 2018

A comprehensive and at times entertaining story of the laws governing London's horse cabs and cabmen.

Garner, Simon, and Stokoe, Giles. Taxi! Frances Lincoln, 2000

A description of the London cab trade, its cabs and drivers; a light-hearted but accurate introduction to the subject for the general reader. H/b, b/w

Georgano, G. N. A History of the London Taxicab. David & Charles, 1972

The first modern generation book on the subject, long out of print. H/b, b/w

Georgano, G. N., and Munro, Bill. The London Taxicab. Shire Books, 2009

A pocket history of the subject. P/b, full colour

May, Trevor. Gondolas and Growlers: The History of the London Horse Cab. Alan Sutton, 1995

An in-depth academic study, but very readable. Out of print. H/b, black & white

May, Trevor. Victorian and Edwardian Horse Cabs. Shire Books, 1999

A pocket version of the above. P/b, b/w. Out of Print

Merkel, Ben, and Monier, Chris. The American Taxi: A Century of Service. Iconografix, 2006

A broad history of a very large subject. P/b, b/w with some colour. Out of Print

Munro, Bill. Carbodies, the Complete Story. Crowood, 1998

The story of the company that became London Taxis International. Out of print H/b, b/w colour centre.

Munro, Bill. A Century of London Taxis. Crowood, 2005

In-depth history of the subject. H/b, b/w with colour centre section. Out of Print

Munro, Bill. Taxi Jubilee - Fifty Years of the Austin FX4 London Taxi. Earlswood Press, 2009. A5 p/b.

A full colour history of the definitive "black cab".

Munro, Bill. London Taxis – a Full History. Earlswood Press, 2005 & 2011

Essentially an update of A Century of London Taxis. P/b, b/w. Out of Print

Munro, Bill. FX4 Black Cab. Haynes, 2012 P/b and H/b, colour

An in-depth, full colour study of the model, from 1958 to 1997. Out of Print

Ward, Rod. Taxi - Purpose-built Cabs in Britain. Malvern House Publications, 2008

Pictures of cabs of all ages from all around the UK. P/b, b/w with some colour

Warren, Philip. The History of the London Cab Trade. Taxi Trade Promotions, 1995

The definitive history of the subject. H/b & p/b, b/w. Out of Print

Warren, Philip, and Linskey, Malcolm. Taxicabs -A Photographic History. Almark, 1976

A wide range of photographs of cabs up to the early 1970s. H/b, b/w. Out of Print.